Collins

easy learning

Counting

Ages 3–5

Carol Medcalf

How to use this book

- Find a quiet, comfortable place to work, away from distractions.

- This book has been written in a logical order, so start at the first page and work your way through.

- Help with reading the instructions where necessary and ensure that your child understands what to do.

- This book is a gentle introduction to counting. You may need to introduce counters or small objects to help your child understand the concepts of adding and subtraction. Try to use the following language as you work through the book together: add, plus, take away, minus, more than, less than, equals, all together, left over, set/s, half.

- If an activity is too difficult for your child then do more of our suggested practical activities (see Activity note) and return to the page when you know that they're likely to achieve it.

- Always end each activity before your child gets tired so that they will be eager to return next time.

- Help and encourage your child to check their own answers as they complete each activity.

- Let your child return to their favourite pages once they have been completed. Talk about the activities they enjoyed and what they have learnt.

Special features of this book:

- **Activity note:** situated at the bottom of every left-hand page, this suggests further activities and encourages discussion about what your child has learnt.

- **Counting panel:** situated at the bottom of every right-hand page, this shows simple additions and subtractions outlined with pictures and in written form. Use this to recap what your child has learnt.

- **Certificate:** the certificate on page 24 should be used to reward your child for their effort and achievement. Remember to give them plenty of praise and encouragement, regardless of how they do.

Published by Collins
An imprint of HarperCollinsPublishers Ltd
The News Building
1 London Bridge Street
London
SE1 9GF

Browse the complete Collins catalogue at
www.collins.co.uk

© HarperCollinsPublishers Ltd 2006
This edition © HarperCollinsPublishers Ltd 2015
10 9 8 7 6 5 4
Printed and bound in Great Britain by Bell and Bain Ltd, Glasgow

ISBN 978-0-00-815152-2

The author asserts the moral right to be identified as the author of this work.

British Library Cataloguing in Publication Data

A Catalogue record for this publication is available from the British Library.

Written by Carol Medcalf
Design and layout by Lodestone Publishing Limited and Contentra Technologies Ltd
Illustrated by Jenny Tulip
Cover image by Kathy Baxendale
Cover design by Sarah Duxbury and Paul Oates
Project managed by Sonia Dawkins

MIX
Paper from responsible sources
FSC
www.fsc.org
FSC™ C007454

Contents

Numbers

Trace the numbers. Count and colour the counters.

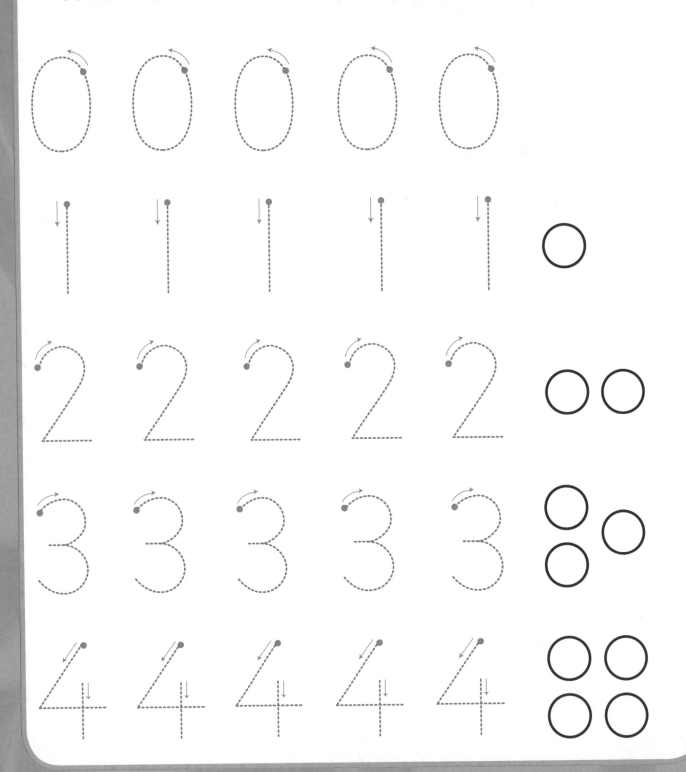

Use this page to recap numbers 1 to 10 and introduce zero. Explain that if you have no counters then you have zero, which is represented by the number 0. You can also show this visually by using building blocks (as used in the counting panel opposite). As you start, explain that you have no blocks and point to the number 0. Then count the blocks as you build from 1 to 10.

5 5 5 5

6 6 6 6

7 7 7 7

8 8 8 8

9 9 9 9

10 10 10

+ = 0 + 1 = 1

5

Counting

Count the pictures in each set. Draw lines to match the set with the correct number.

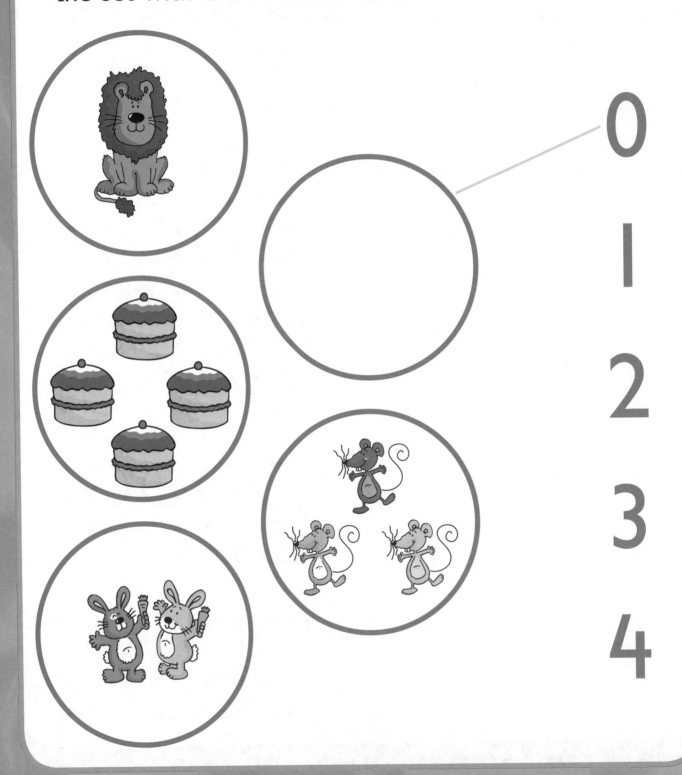

0

1

2

3

4

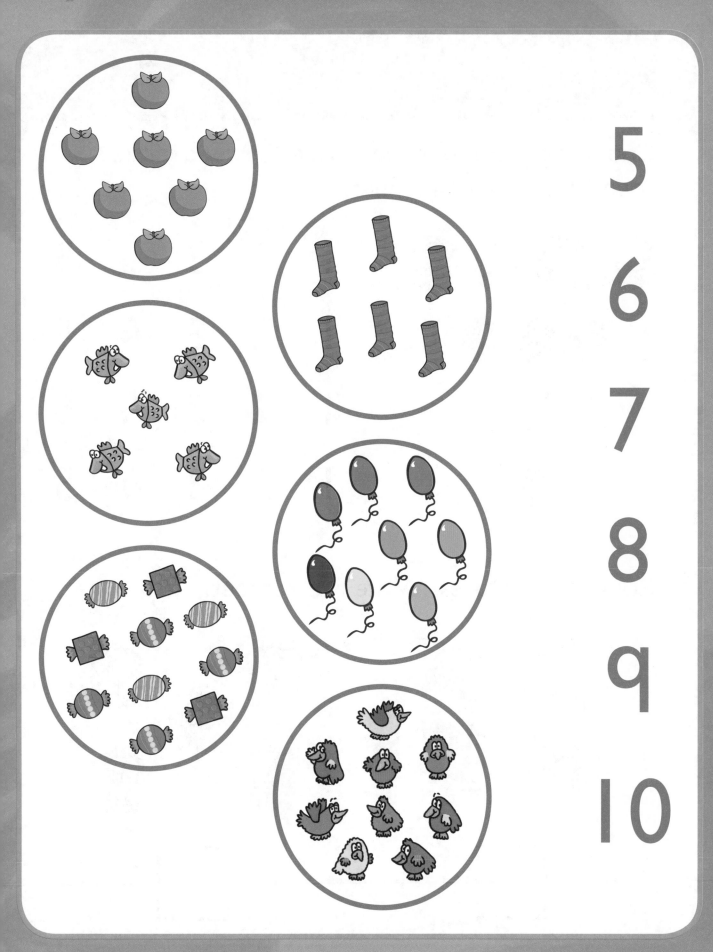

5
6
7
8
q
10

 + =   1 + 1 = 2

7

How many?

- Count the pictures in each row. Draw a circle round the correct number.

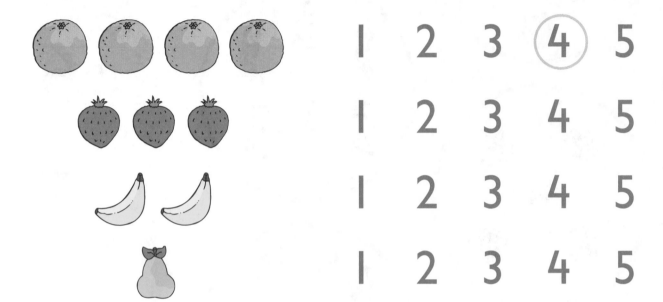

1	2	3	④	5
1	2	3	4	5
1	2	3	4	5
1	2	3	4	5

- Count the pictures. Write the number.

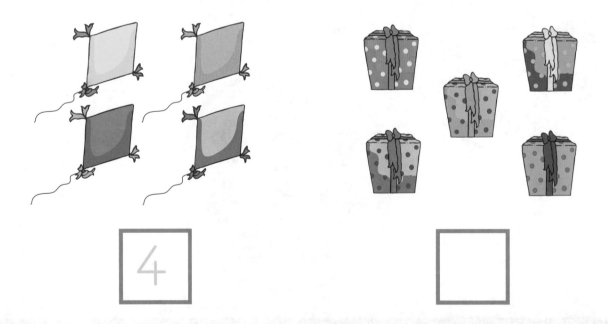

4

How many altogether?

● How many of these can you count in the big picture?
  Write the number.

More and less

- Who has more balloons? (✔)

- Who has less presents? (✔)

Try to count together during everyday experiences. When you are outside look and say:
'Look at that bird, there is another, that makes two' or 'How many swings are there
altogether?' Try and make it a normal part of your day.

Adding 1

● Draw one more spider. How many are there altogether? Write the number.

● Count each set. Say the sum out loud.

 and makes

 +  =    1 + 3 = 4

Adding 2

● Finish the sum. Draw the answer.

and   makes

● Count each set. Add them together. Write the total.

and   makes

When adding, encourage your child to touch each picture as they count.
Always count slowly.

Adding 3

● Count each set. Say the sum out loud.

● Draw 3 more balls. Add them together. Write the total.

and   makes [ ]

□ + ⬛⬛ = ⬛⬛⬛   1 + 4 = 5

Adding 4

Write the numbers in the boxes to make the totals.

1 + 4 = ☐

2 + 4 = ☐

Count and add together everyday familiar objects, such as coins, buttons and building bricks.
Use mathematical language such as 'plus', 'add' and 'equals'.

Adding 5

● Colour 5 more flags.

How many flags are there altogether?

● Count the sandwiches and write the sum.

│ │ + │ │ = │ │

 – =   5 – 1 = 4

15

Adding practice

- Finish the sum. Draw the answer.

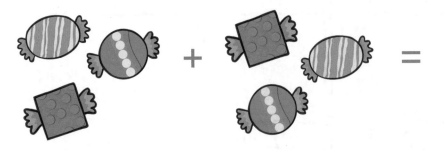

- Say the sum out loud. Draw a (circle) round the correct answer.

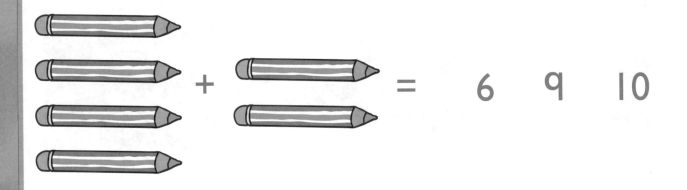

$$+ \quad = \quad 6 \quad 9 \quad 10$$

Save 10 plastic bottles and put labels on them from 1 to 10. Put them on a wall or table and count them. Knock one bottle off and count again. Ask: 'How many are left?' and then say the sum: '10 take away 1 is 9'. Sing the song 'Ten green bottles' together.

Take away 1

- How many bottles are left on the wall? Write the number.

10 bottles take away 1 bottle leaves ☐ bottles.

Now write the sum.

☐ – ☐ = ☐

5 – 2 = 3

Take away 2

● Count the socks. Cross 2 out. How many are left?

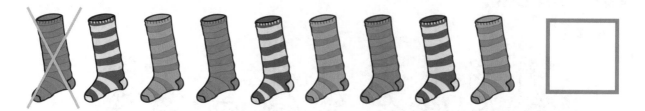

● Count the children in the picture. How many are running away? How many are left?

Now finish the sum.

7 − ☐ = ☐

Count and take away when eating. Say: 'You have 6 grapes. If we take away 1 (as they eat it), how many are left?'

Take away 3

Write the total.

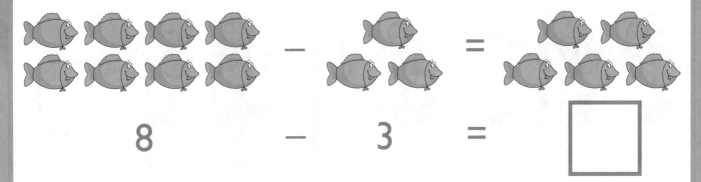

$$8 \quad - \quad 3 \quad = \quad \boxed{}$$

Count the birds in the picture. How many are flying away? How many are left?

Now finish the sum.

$$10 \quad - \quad \boxed{} \quad = \quad \boxed{}$$

5 − 3 = 2

Take away 4

- Count the flowers. Cross 4 out. How many are left?

Now finish the sum.

$$7 - \boxed{} = \boxed{}$$

- Finish the sum. Draw the answer.

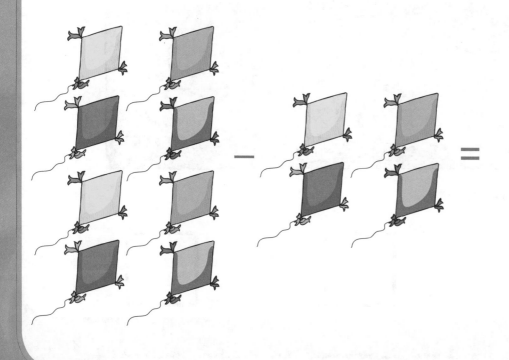

Take away 5

● Count the apples on the tree.

Five apples fall off.

How many apples are left on the tree? ☐

Now write the sum.

☐ − ☐ = ☐

= ▢   5 − 4 = 1

Take away practice

● Count the pictures. Cover up the ones that you are taking away. How many are left?

7 take away 3 is

7 take away 1 is

5 take away 2 is

5 take away 5 is

8 – 4 =

8 – 2 =

Discuss different ways that totals are made: 4 + 1 makes 5 and 3 + 2 makes 5, 5 – 2 leaves 3 and 6 – 3 leaves 3.

Counting practice

● How many teddies are left in the bed? Write the number.

10 teddies take away 3 teddies leaves ☐ teddies.

Now finish the sum.

10 – 3 = ☐

 = 5 – 5 = 0

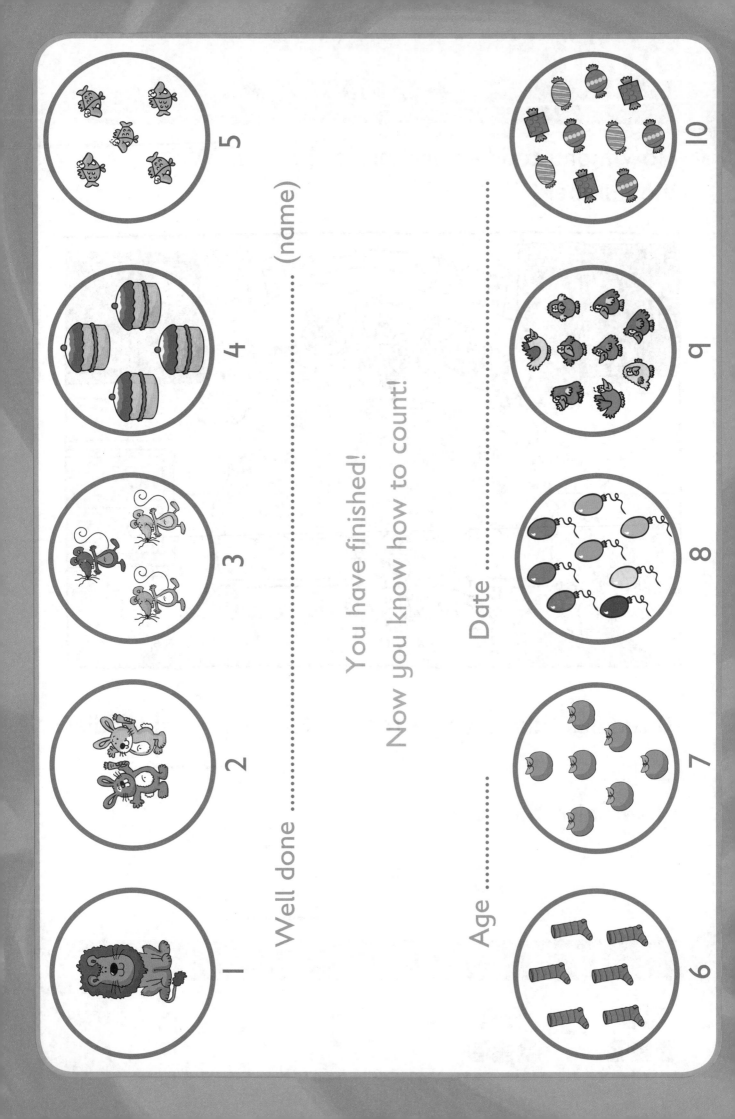

1

2

3

4

5

Well done .... (name)

You have finished!
Now you know how to count!

Age ....

Date ....

6

7

8

9

10